21st Century Skills Library

INSIDE U.S. ELECTIONS

WHAT IS A PRIMARY?

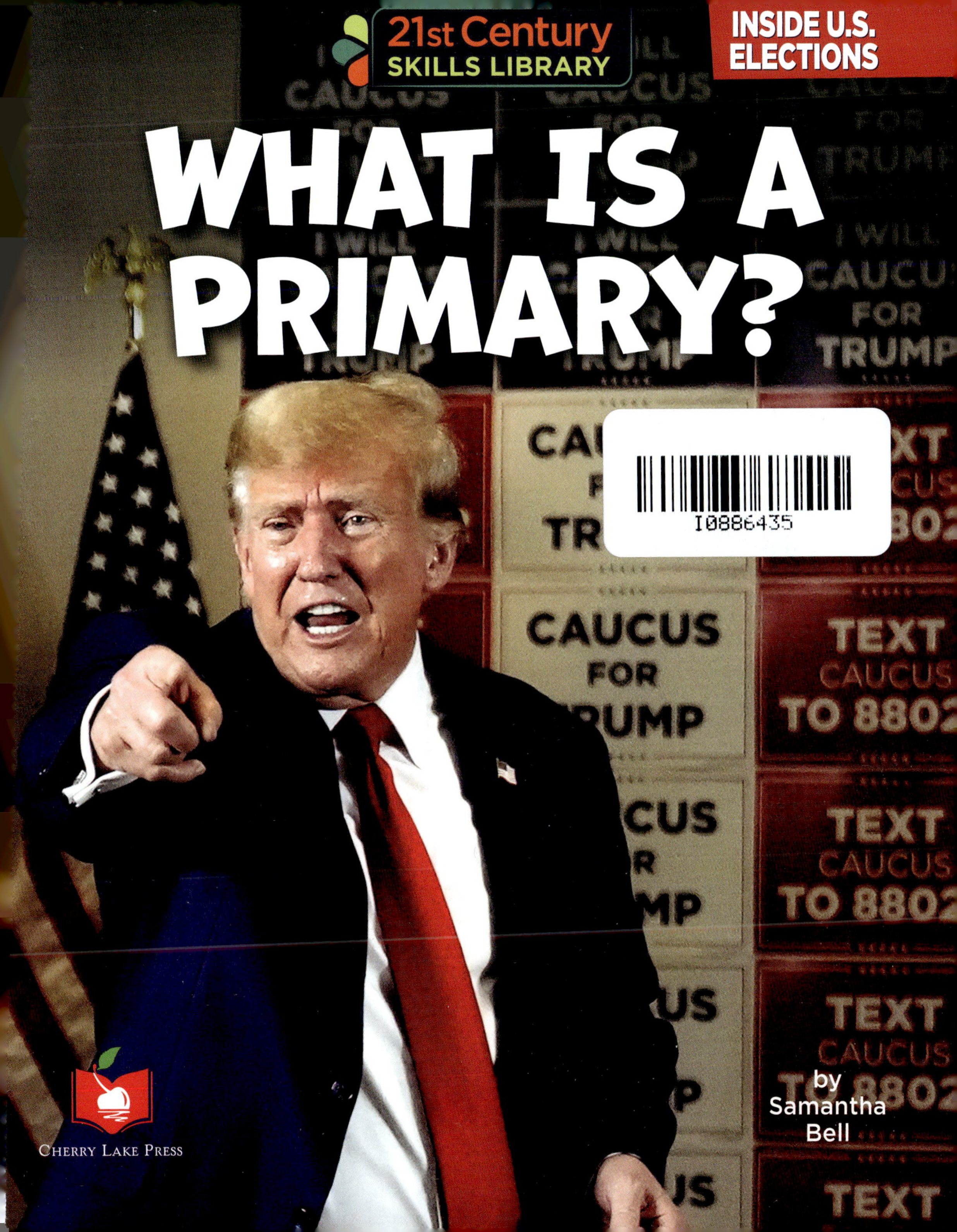

by Samantha Bell

Cherry Lake Press

Cherry Lake Press

Published in the United States of America by
Cherry Lake Publishing Group
Ann Arbor, Michigan
www.cherrylakepublishing.com

Reading Adviser: Beth Walker Gambro, MS, Ed., Reading Consultant, Yorkville, IL

Content Adviser: Mark Richards, Ph.D., Professor, Dept. of Political Science, Grand Valley State University, Allendale, MI

Photo Credits: © AP Photo/Andrew Harnik, cover, title page; Prints and Photographs Division, Library of Congress, 5; Prints and Photographs Division, Library of Congress, 6; Nast, Thomas, 1840-1902, artist, Public domain, 7; Los Angeles Daily News, CC BY 4.0 via Wikimedia Commons, 8; Prints and Photographs Division, Library of Congress, 10; Rbreidbrown, CC BY-SA 4.0 via Wikimedia Commons, 13; © Varga Jozsef Zoltan/Shutterstock, 14; © Chris Manning/Shutterstock, 15; © Trevor Bexon/Shutterstock, 17; K. Farabaugh/VOA, Public domain, via Wikimedia Commons, 18; © AnAdventureADay/Shutterstock, 21; roanokecollege, CC BY 2.0 via Wikimedia Commons, 23; © Ilya B. Mirman/Shutterstock, 24; © Andrew Cline/Shutterstock, 25; © Oscar Ivan Lopez/Shutterstock, 26; © Andrew Cline/ Shutterstock, 29; New Hampshire. Dept. of State, No restrictions, via Wikimedia Commons, 30; Warren K. Leffler, U.S. News & World Report Magazine, Public domain, via Wikimedia Commons, 31; Unknown, dedicated to Bettmann Archive, Public domain, via Wikimedia Commons, 32; Panoramic Photographs, Prints and Photographs Division, Library of Congress, 37; Leffler, Warren K., U.S. News & World Report Magazine Photograph Collection, Prints and Photographs Division, Library of Congress, 39; United States Information Agency, Public domain, via Wikimedia Commons, 40; Anthony Quintano from Westminster, United States, CC BY 2.0 via Wikimedia Commons, 41; © mark reinstein/Shutterstock, 42; © Carol M. Highsmith, Public domain, via Wikimedia Commons, 43

Cherry Lake Press is an imprint of Cherry Lake Publishing Group.

Library of Congress Cataloging-in-Publication Data has been filed and is available at catalog.loc.gov

Printed in the United States of America

CONTENTS

CHAPTER 1

HOW PRIMARIES BEGAN

Primary elections are state elections. They are also known as primaries. Most primaries focus on candidates from one of the two main political parties. These are the Democratic and Republican Parties. Each party has its own primaries.

People can vote in one of the primaries. They vote for the candidate they want to represent the party. The winning candidate becomes the party's **nominee**. They will run against the other party's nominee in the general election.

RULING THE PARTY

Primaries were not always part of the election process. In the early 1800s, candidates were chosen by political **caucuses**. These were small meetings

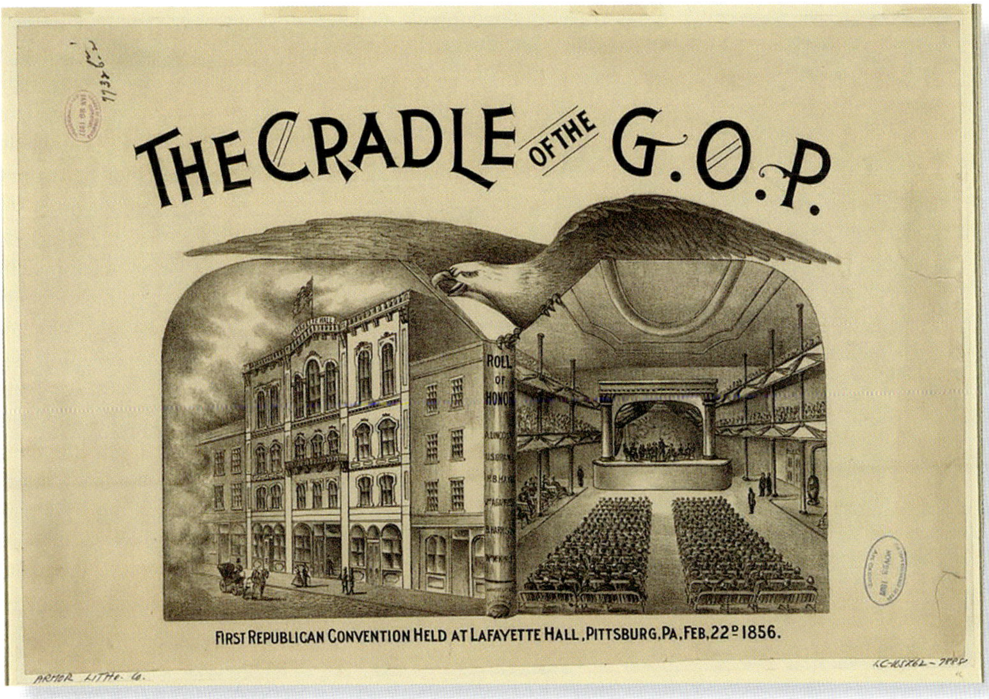

The first Republican Convention was in 1856 in Pittsburgh, Pennsylvania.

among the party leaders. These leaders chose the candidates who would run for president.

The first political **conventions** were held in 1831 and 1832. Each state sent **delegates** to the conventions. A delegate is a representative of the party. The delegates voted for candidates. Their votes decided the party's nominee. By the mid-1800s, the conventions had become the main way parties chose their candidates.

Franklin Pierce went on to become the
14th president of the United States.

The party leaders were known as party bosses. Over time, they became very powerful. They often chose the delegates themselves. That way, they could influence the delegates. They could control their votes at the conventions.

The candidate who won the vote ran for president. This is called winning the nomination. The voting was done in rounds. The rounds continued until someone won. It often took many rounds to win a nomination. For example, in 1852, Democrats took 49 tries before nominating Franklin Pierce.

Party bosses took control at the conventions. The voting often took a long time. While delegates were voting, some of the party bosses made deals. They gave the delegates money and secured their votes. The delegates voted the way the bosses told them. The party bosses were still controlling who the nominees would be.

A TIME FOR CHANGE

Around 1890, people wanted to change the political process. They didn't want the party bosses to be in

William "Boss" Tweed was the party boss at Tammany Hall. It was a Democratic Party group.

In 1952, Adlai Stevenson connected with his supporters through the media. It worked! He won the Democratic nomination for president. But Dwight D. Eisenhower won the presidency.

control anymore. In the years that followed, the states passed new laws about elections. They began to hold primaries. Then the voters could select the delegates. This way, the voters had more say in who the candidates would be. By 1916, 25 states had presidential primaries.

More changes came in the 1940s. Most people had radios. Some even had televisions. Candidates began using the airwaves. They could get their message directly to the voters. Some candidates were not well-known. But now they had a chance to be in the primaries. They didn't have to depend on party leaders for support.

In 1952, Democratic candidate Adlai Stevenson used the media to connect with voters. He wasn't the choice of the party leaders. But he won state primaries. He went on to win the nomination.

Before the 1960s, no one knew for sure which candidate would win the nomination. The delegates came to the convention. The party bosses would try to influence the votes. But no one was certain who the delegates would vote for. They just kept voting until a candidate received a **majority** of votes.

But in 1960, the system changed. John F. Kennedy ran for the Democratic nomination. The leading candidates were Lyndon B. Johnson and Hubert Humphrey. The party leaders preferred Johnson, so he didn't enter any primaries. Humphrey skipped the early ones. But Kennedy competed and won the most votes. He went on to win the nomination at the convention. This meant the party leaders were no longer in control.

Despite the protests and violence happening outside, the 1968 Democratic National Convention went on. Some convention delegates criticized Chicago's handling of the protests in their speeches.

The next important change came in 1968. That year, the Democratic convention was held in Chicago, Illinois. Thousands of protestors came to the convention. They were angry about the Vietnam War (1954–1975). People began fighting in the streets. There were riots and bloodshed. The protestors, police, and even bystanders got involved. Hubert Humphrey was nominated. But everything seemed out of control.

Later that year, Republicans met for their convention in Miami, Florida. They thought about the Democrats in Chicago. The Republican convention was well-planned and organized. Later conventions copied it. They wanted to avoid the kind of trouble the Democrats had.

TRUE STORY: WON WITH ONE PRIMARY

In 1912, Theodore Roosevelt ran for a third term as president. He planned to run as a Republican. His opponent was President William Howard Taft. Most states were controlled by party bosses. But some states had primaries. This gave the voters a say in the process.

Taft and Roosevelt had once been friends. But the election was full of personal attacks. Roosevelt campaigned hard. He won almost all the primaries. Taft won only one primary. But the party bosses supported Taft. They chose most of the delegates at the convention. In the end, Taft became the Republican nominee. However, he lost the election to Democrat Woodrow Wilson.

CHAPTER 2

TYPES OF PRIMARIES

Today, delegates still represent their party at national conventions. They still vote for the candidate they want to run for president. But the system has changed.

Now, rules ensure delegates will be accurately representing the wishes of the people from their political party and state. Each major party has a set number of delegates based on the state's population. There are different ways to decide which candidate these delegates vote for at the national conventions.

Depending on the state, delegates may be chosen to represent a certain candidate through either a primary or a caucus. Primaries are usually run by state governments. Caucuses are run by political parties.

In a primary, people simply go to vote. They mark a **ballot** for their choice of candidate. The states make

The Iowa caucuses are the first primary event in every election year. They take place in January.

their own rules for their primaries, including who can participate.

Caucuses are meetings that voters attend. They involve a lot of **debate** and discussions. The party makes the rules for the caucus. These include when and where the meetings will take place.

VOTING AT THE PRIMARIES

Primaries are held 5 to 9 months before the presidential election. During the primaries, voters go to the polling place. They vote for their preferred candidate. After the primary is over, the state considers the results of the vote. Then it decides which

Donald Trump won the 2024 Iowa caucuses for the Republican Party.

candidates will win the allotted number of delegates for each party.

There are different types of primaries. The states decide which kind to use. A voter may be **eligible** to vote in more than one party's primary. But they may participate in only one.

Some states have open primaries. Any registered voter can vote in an open primary. It doesn't matter which party they belong to. They don't even have to belong to a party at all. Voters choose which party's ballot they will use. They may vote for someone in their own party. Or they may vote for a candidate in another party. This system gives voters the most freedom.

Trump spoke in Clive, Iowa, at the 2024 Iowa caucuses.

In a closed primary, only voters registered with that party can vote. For example, voters registered as Democrats can vote in the Democratic primary. Those registered as Republicans can vote in the Republican primary. But this system prevents **independents** from voting. Independents are voters who aren't registered with a party. They can't participate in any of the closed primaries.

In semi-closed primaries, political parties may allow independents to vote. If so, then independents can choose to vote in either the Democratic or Republican primary. But this rule can change from year to year. Sometimes independents are able to vote. Other times, they may not. But people registered with a party can still vote in their party's primary.

MEETING AT THE CAUCUSES

Like primaries, caucuses can be open or closed. Or they can be a combination of the two. But there are some major differences. Primaries are held throughout a state. During a primary, voters go to

Many candidates hold rallies leading up to primaries and caucuses. President Joe Biden held a rally before the Nevada primary and caucuses.

their polling places. They cast their ballots. But caucuses are held at the local level. They are meetings voters can attend.

The party announces the date, time, and location of the caucus. Any voter registered with the party may go. Unlike primaries, caucuses allow voters to discuss the candidates. Voters can try to win more votes for their favorite candidate. They can discuss campaign issues, such as the economy, education, or crime. They also might discuss immigration or foreign policy.

Caucuses have different ways of choosing candidates. Some caucuses choose them by secret ballot. Other caucuses require voters to divide into groups. These are based on the candidate they support. Some voters are undecided. They form their own group.

Each candidate's group gives speeches. They try to convince others to join their group. Each group needs to have at least 15 percent of the voters. If they don't, the voters must join another group. After more discussion and debate, a vote is taken. The vote determines which candidate's delegates will go to the convention.

This process can take a lot of time. A caucus can last for hours. This may prevent many voters from participating. They may not be able to attend such a

Many voters gather at a caucus.

long meeting. Some may have to work. Others may have to care for children or other family members.

Primaries are usually much shorter. Over the years, most states have changed from caucuses to primaries. Many of these states have switched since 2016. Today, only some states still use caucuses.

PERSPECTIVES: PLAYING FAIR

Some people are concerned about open primaries. They worry that people won't vote for their preferred candidate. Instead, they might vote to harm the other party. This is called party raiding. One party schemes to vote in the other party's primary.

People have different reasons for party raiding. They might vote for a candidate whom the regular voters of that primary don't support. Or they may vote for a weaker candidate. That way, their candidate has an easier time running against them in the general election. However, many people see this as dishonest. It's not a fair way to influence an election.

CHAPTER 3

PRIMARY ELECTION PROCESS

States hold primaries for most public offices. Presidential primaries are the most well-known. During primaries, people vote for the candidates they prefer. The primaries help narrow down the number of candidates.

The state where the primary is held considers the results of the vote. Then the state decides how many delegates will attend the Democratic National Convention. It decides how many will attend the Republican National Convention. It decides which candidates these delegates will represent at each convention.

The states control the primaries. They also control how the delegates are chosen. But states don't make choices in the same way. There can be major differences from state to state and from year to year.

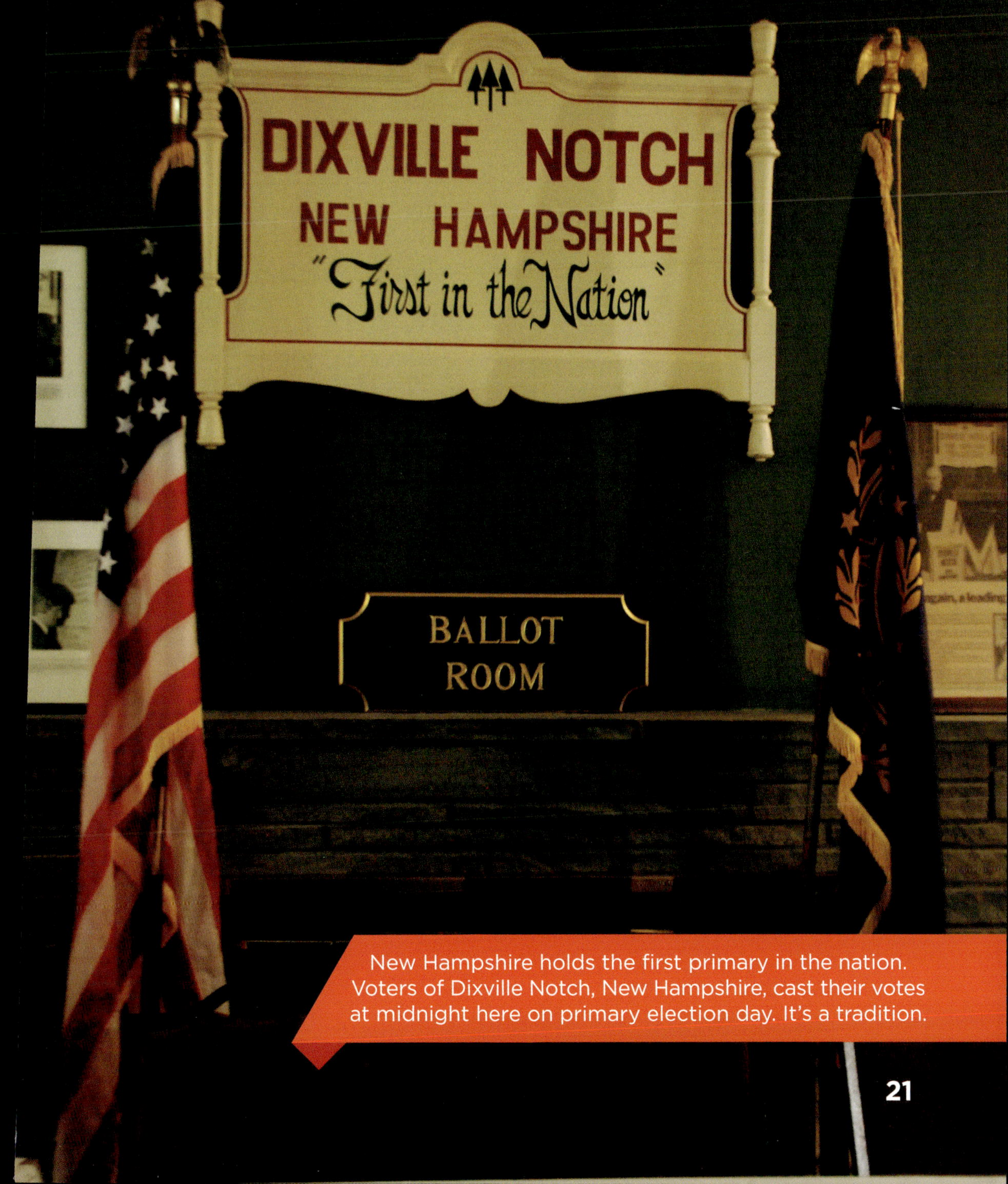

New Hampshire holds the first primary in the nation. Voters of Dixville Notch, New Hampshire, cast their votes at midnight here on primary election day. It's a tradition.

THE DELEGATES

Each political party has its own rules for selecting delegates. The states and U.S. **territories** have their own rules too. The rules determine who is qualified to be a delegate. The rules also decide how many delegates each state will have.

For Democrats, any person who is registered to vote as a Democrat can become a delegate. The party provides education and training programs. Each state has an equal number of men and women delegates.

For Republicans, most delegates are chosen by state conventions or committees. These are made up of elected officials and volunteers. They may also include local **activists**. The number of delegates for each state is based on its size.

In both parties, most delegates are committed to vote for a certain candidate. Republicans call these people "bound" delegates. Democrats call them "pledged" delegates.

Each party also has delegates who are not committed to a candidate. Republicans call

Senator Joe Lieberman (1942–2024), registered as a Democrat, lost his superdelegate status in 2008 when he endorsed a Republican candidate.

them “unbound” delegates. Democrats call them “unpledged” delegates. These delegates can vote for any candidate they want. They can also switch their support of a candidate at any time.

Unpledged Democratic delegates are sometimes called superdelegates. They are also called automatic delegates. This is because their position in the party automatically makes them a delegate. They include members of Congress and state governors. They also include former presidents and vice presidents.

WINNING VOTES, WINNING DELEGATES

In a primary or caucus, one candidate will win more individual votes. This is called the popular vote. But that doesn't mean they have won the primary. The state still needs to award the delegates. Many states require that candidates earn a certain number of votes just to qualify for any delegates.

The two major parties have different ways of awarding delegates. This varies from state to state

In the 2024 New Hampshire Republican primary, Donald Trump won more of the popular vote. With the proportional method in New Hampshire, he got 13 delegates, and Nikki Haley got 9.

The proportional method was also used in the 2024 South Carolina Republican primaries. Donald Trump gained 47 delegates and Nikki Haley gained 3 delegates.

and party to party. One method is winner-take-all. This means that whoever receives the most votes in the primary wins every delegate.

Another method is the proportional method. With this method, the number of delegates the candidate wins depends on the number of votes they receive. The delegates are awarded in proportion to the votes. For example, a candidate might win 40 percent of the vote. They then receive 40 percent of the delegates.

In the 2024 Michigan primary, Joe Biden gained 115 delegates. "Uncommitted" gained 2 delegates.

In some states, Republicans use the proportional method. In others, they use the winner-take-all method. Sometimes they use a mix of both methods. The Democratic Party always uses a proportional method. The winner is the candidate who gets a majority of delegates.

TRUE STORY: GETTING TO THE GENERAL ELECTION

In 1980, John B. Anderson ran for the Republican nomination. He lost to Ronald Reagan in the primaries. But Anderson didn't give up. He couldn't participate in the general election as a Republican. But he could participate as an independent. He ran against Reagan and the Democratic candidate, President Jimmy Carter.

During the election, Anderson wanted to join a debate. Carter refused to debate him. But Reagan agreed. It was the first time a third-party candidate debated a major-party candidate on TV. Anderson lost the general election. But he still received about 7 percent of the vote. He had about 5.7 million supporters.

CHAPTER 4

FIRST STEPS: IOWA AND NEW HAMPSHIRE

The first major event of a presidential election year is the Iowa caucuses. Democrats and Republicans gather at the caucuses. They listen to speeches from a candidate's supporters. Then they vote for their favorite candidate. The second major event is the New Hampshire primary. It is the first primary of the election season.

Iowa and New Hampshire have held the first election events for many years. Some voters think they should not matter that much. These states don't have large populations. Many other states have more delegates.

However, Iowa and New Hampshire have traditionally received a lot of attention. The national news covers the results. For the first time, people can

Republican primary candidate Ron DeSantis held a rally leading up to the 2024 New Hampshire primary. He dropped out of the primary race on January 21, 2024.

see where real voters stand. Candidates who do well receive a boost in their campaigns. They get more positive attention from the media. Voters often become more confident in their chosen candidates.

WHY IOWA AND NEW HAMPSHIRE?

New Hampshire has held the first primary since the 1920s. The Iowa caucus began in 1968. At this

The New Hampshire State House in Concord, New Hampshire, in the 1920s, when New Hampshire started holding the first primary in the nation

When speakers criticized the Chicago Police Department's handling of the 1968 Democratic convention protests, Richard M. Daley reacted in the crowd. His father was the mayor.

time, the party bosses still controlled the nominating process.

The 1968 Democratic convention was marked with violence. People outside were protesting the Vietnam War. The party bosses chose Hubert Humphrey as the party's nominee. He didn't even run in the primaries. Humphrey supported the war. The violence grew worse after his nomination.

At the next convention in 1972, Democratic officials wanted to avoid the same situation.

George McGovern won 37.5 percent of the popular vote in the 1972 election. Richard Nixon won the presidency.

They changed the nominating process. They wanted to include more voters.

Iowa has a complex election process. First, citizens hold caucuses. Then they have county, district, and state conventions. It was important that Iowa started early. Iowa had to choose a date in January. It became the first caucus of the year.

One of the Democratic candidates in 1972 was George McGovern. He wasn't well-known. His opponent was already gaining support in New Hampshire. McGovern decided to focus on Iowa, as it was the first of the primary election events.

He spent a lot of time and resources campaigning in Iowa. He placed second in the election. But it was enough to boost his campaign. McGovern eventually won the party's nomination.

Republicans saw how much influence Iowa had. They changed their schedule for the next presidential election. That year, the Republicans held their caucuses in Iowa on the same day. They wanted to take advantage of the impact of Iowa too.

The next candidate to test the effect of the Iowa caucuses was Jimmy Carter. He began campaigning in Iowa in 1975. He spent a lot of time talking with people. He visited small towns. He went to local events. He came in second in the 1976 Iowa caucuses. The media picked up on his success. He used this **momentum** to win the nomination and later the presidency. Both parties used his strategy in future campaigns.

STAYING IN FRONT

New Hampshire has protected its position with a new law. The law allows it to change its primary date. That

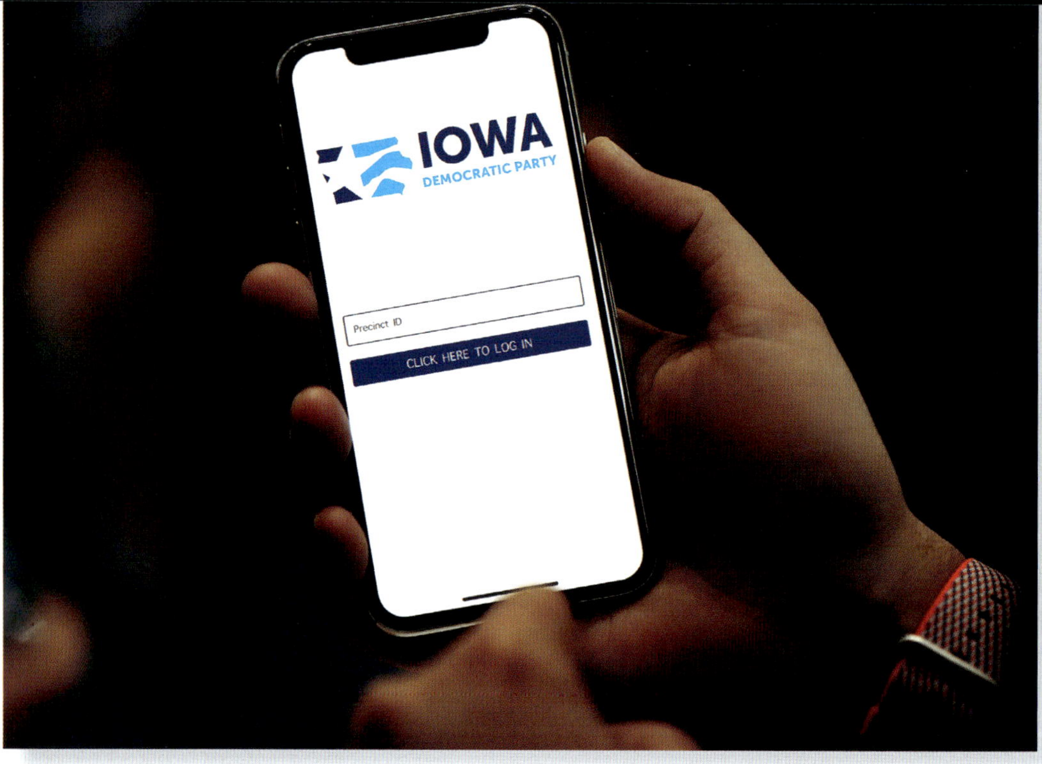

Iowa's Democratic Party utilized an app for the Iowa caucuses. Political parties and campaigns often try to reach more voters through the use of technology.

way, New Hampshire's primary can always be held one week earlier than any other primary.

The Democratic and Republican parties historically made sure New Hampshire would be first. They would have punished other states for holding any earlier elections. However, in 2024, New Hampshire was pushed to the #2 spot.

Iowa and New Hampshire don't always pick the winner. In 2020, Joe Biden came in fourth in Iowa.

He came in fifth in New Hampshire. Then he went on to win the nomination and the presidency. But these two states are still important to campaigns. They often help them gain momentum as they move into the rest of the primaries.

SPOTLIGHT ON: SUPER TUESDAY

In the 1980s, Alabama, Georgia, and Florida all held their primaries on the same day. It became known as Super Tuesday. Since then, more than 10 other states have joined. It is the single biggest voting day in the primaries.

Super Tuesday is held in February or March. It comes after the Iowa and New Hampshire contests. The primaries cover different geographic regions. It is a good opportunity for candidates to gain more delegates. Many experts believe Super Tuesday can strongly affect the outcome of a race.

CHAPTER 5

NATIONAL CONVENTIONS

Like political parties, presidential nominating conventions are not mentioned in the Constitution. But they are an important part of American politics. National conventions are held every 4 years. Each party holds its own conventions.

Parties choose convention sites several years in advance. The cities where the conventions are held must have enough facilities. They need hotels and meeting halls for thousands of people. Sometimes a convention renominates a current president. Then the president usually gets to choose the location.

A convention often lasts 4 days. Delegates to the convention represent all 50 states. There are also delegates representing the District of Columbia and several U.S. territories.

The 1920 Republican National Convention in Chicago, Illinois

THE VOTES

At conventions, delegates go through a regular set of procedures. These involve several votes. The first vote deals with who is included at the convention. The next vote covers the rules. After that, there's a vote to approve the platform. The last vote is the roll-call vote. This is the vote that determines the party's nominee.

When the first round of voting begins, all of the pledged or bound delegates vote. They must vote for a certain candidate. This is based on the results of their state primary or caucus. This requirement lasts at least through the first round of voting. But in the second round, they may be free to vote for any candidate in their party. This depends on state and party rules.

Unpledged and unbound delegates may support any candidate from their party. In the Democratic Party, these delegates may not be able to vote right away. If the race is close, they must wait until the second round to vote. This way, they don't have too much power. For Republicans, only a small number of delegates are unbound. They are free to vote anytime.

A candidate must win a majority of the votes to become the nominee. Sometimes there isn't any **controversy**. There is a clear winner in the primaries. The nominee has been decided before the convention.

Sometimes there is a brokered convention. This is when there is no clear winner after the first vote.

This is Shirley Chisholm at the 1972 Democratic National Convention. She was the first Black woman to run for the Democratic Party's bid for president. She didn't win but still made history.

Then the delegates vote again. This time, all of the pledged delegates may vote. This way, they can eventually select a nominee. The delegates continue with rounds of voting. Finally, a candidate has enough votes. These types of conventions are rare. The last one occurred in 1952.

Other times, there can be a contested convention. This is when one of the candidates has done well. But they have not done well enough to win on the first vote.

Hubert Humphrey won the Democratic bid for president at the 1968 Democratic National Convention. Many delegates shouted, "No! No!" when he was chosen.

Most of the time, when the party's nominee for president is announced, there is a lot of celebration.

Another candidate from the party then steps in. This candidate tries to convince delegates to vote for them instead.

WINNING THE NOMINATION

When a candidate wins the vote, they become the party's nominee. They will run for the party in the general election. This election decides who the president will be for the next 4 years.

After the nominee wins, they give an acceptance speech. The speech is an important moment in the campaign. The nominee explains their vision.

In Trump's 2016 Republican National Convention nominee acceptance speech, he said, "We will lead our country back to safety, prosperity, and peace."

They communicate their values. They try to gain support from other candidates and party members.

Acceptance speeches can be powerful. The nominees are careful about the words they use. They try to appeal to voters' emotions. It is an opportunity to connect with voters and win them over.

The national conventions have changed a lot over time. They have become more democratic. When voters participate, they can make their voices heard.

FUN FACTS: THE BALLOON DROP

Many conventions end with thousands of balloons. The tradition began at the 1932 Republican convention. Balloons fell again at the 1956 convention. Now they are used at both parties' conventions. But not every balloon drop goes as planned. In 1980, the Democratic balloon drop **malfunctioned**. It became one of the biggest stories of the convention.

ACTIVITY

RESEARCH IT!

Do some research about your state's most recent presidential primaries. Ask your parent, teacher, or another trusted adult to help you find the information online. Then answer the following questions:

About Your State
What state do you live in?
Does your state have primaries or caucuses?
On what date were the most recent primaries or caucuses held? Were they part of Super Tuesday?

About the Republicans
Who were the Republican candidates?
What percentage of the popular vote did each one receive?
Who won your state's primary?
Did that person become the party's nominee?

About the Democrats
Who were the Democratic candidates?
What percentage of the popular vote did each one receive?
Who won your state's primary?
Did that person become the party's nominee?

You can also ask the adult helping you who they voted for.
How did their candidate do?

GLOSSARY

activists (AK-tih-vihsts) people who work for political or social change

ballot (BA-luht) piece of paper on which voters enter their choices

caucuses (KAW-kuhs-ez) a meeting of members of one political party to decide on candidates or policies

controversy (KAHN-truh-vur-see) discussion and argument about something, often involving strong feelings of anger

conventions (kuhn-VEN-shuhnz) large meetings or conferences, especially of members of a political party

debate (dih-BAYT) a discussion between two people or groups on an important subject

delegates (DEH-lih-guhts) people from each state who represent a certain candidate and attend their party's national convention

eligible (EH-luh-juh-buhl) qualified

independents (in-duh-PEN-duhntz) voters who aren't members of any political party

malfunctioned (mal-FUHNK-shuhnd) failed to operate properly

majority (muh-JOR-uh-tee) more than half of the total number or amount

momentum (moh-MEN-tuhm) strength or force gained by a series of events

nominee (nah-muh-NEE) a person who is formally entered as a candidate for an office

territories (TER-uh-tor-eez) areas governed by or under the protection of another country

TO LEARN MORE

BOOKS

Haynes, Danielle. *Presidential Primaries and Caucuses*. New York: PowerKids Press, 2020.

Katzman, Rebecca. *Your Vote Matters: How We Elect the US President*. New York: Scholastic, Inc., 2024.

Wesgate, Kathryn. *Primaries and Caucuses*. New York: Gareth Stevens Publishing, 2021.

WEBSITES

Search these online sources with an adult:

"Election of the President and Vice President: Primary Election." Ben's Guide.

"How The Iowa Caucus Works, In 2 Minutes (Starring Legos)." Vermont Public.

"Primaries and Caucuses." Time for Kids.

INDEX

ABOUT THE AUTHOR

Samantha Bell was born and raised near Orlando, Florida. She grew up in a family of eight kids and all kinds of pets, including goats, chickens, cats, dogs, rabbits, horses, parakeets, hamsters, guinea pigs, a monkey, a raccoon, and a coatimundi. She now lives with her family in the foothills of the Blue Ridge Mountains, where she enjoys hiking, painting, and snuggling with their cats, Pocket, Pebble, and Mr. Tree-Tree Triggers.